Full STEAM Ahead!
Engineering Everywhere

What Is the Best Solution?

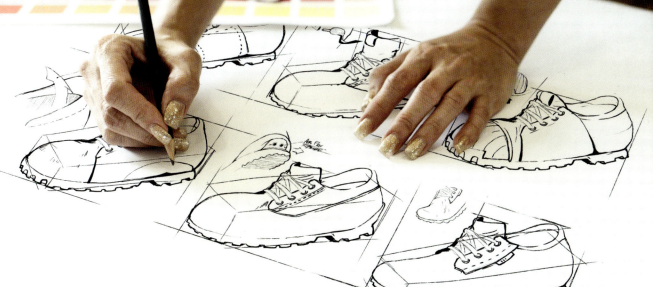

Robin Johnson

CRABTREE PUBLISHING COMPANY
WWW.CRABTREEBOOKS.COM

Title-Specific Learning Objectives:

Readers will:

- Explain that a problem can have many solutions, and that engineers find the best solution to a problem.
- Describe different solutions and how they are found.
- Ask questions about key details in the text, and use evidence to help find answers for their questions.

High-frequency words (grade one) a, an, and, are, have, is, they, to, you	Academic vocabulary brainstorm, creative thinking, design, electric car, energy, model, needs, pollutes, solution

Before, During, and After Reading Prompts:

Activate Prior Knowledge and Make Predictions:

Have children activate their prior knowledge by brainstorming answers to the following questions in groups or in a Think-Pair-Share format.

- What is a solution? Can you name an example?
- Can you think of a time you found a solution?
- What kinds of solutions do engineers find?

During Reading:

After reading pages 8 and 9, ask children to consider solutions that help them meet their needs. Encourage text-to-self connections as you discuss.

After Reading:

Encourage children to notice solutions in the classroom or at home. Have children work in groups to make a chart that sorts the solutions into the following categories: meets a need, makes life safer, makes life easier, makes life more fun.

Have children display their charts and invite peers to view the charts. Then, discuss other solutions that might have worked to achieve the same goal. For example, is an alarm clock the only solution that makes it easier to get to school on time? Discuss how there are many solutions to the same problem. Which solutions work best for them?

Author: Robin Johnson

Series Development: Reagan Miller

Editor: Janine Deschenes

Proofreader: Melissa Boyce

STEAM Notes for Educators: Janine Deschenes

Guided Reading Leveling: Publishing Solutions Group

Cover, Interior Design, and Prepress: Samara Parent

Photo research: Robin Johnson and Samara Parent

Production coordinator: Katherine Berti

Photographs:
Alamy: Dino Fracchia: p. 13 (t); PA Images: p. 19; Gado Reportage: p. 20
iStock: zoranm: p. 15
Shutterstock: Kevin M. McCarthy: p. 16 (r); Michalakis Ppalis: p. 18; oconnelll: p. 21
All other photographs by Shutterstock

Library and Archives Canada Cataloguing in Publication

Title: What is the best solution? / Robin Johnson.
Names: Johnson, Robin (Robin R.), author.
Description: Series statement: Full STEAM ahead! | Includes index.
Identifiers: Canadiana (print) 20190133740 |
  Canadiana (ebook) 20190133767 |
  ISBN 9780778764595 (softcover) |
  ISBN 9780778764090 (hardcover) |
  ISBN 9781427123619 (HTML)
Subjects: LCSH: Engineering—Juvenile literature. |
  LCSH: Engineering—Methodology—Juvenile literature. |
  LCSH: Problem solving—Juvenile literature. |
  LCSH: Creative thinking—Juvenile literature.
Classification: LCC TA149 .J64 2019 | DDC j620—dc23

Library of Congress Cataloging-in-Publication Data

Names: Johnson, Robin, author.
Title: What is the best solution? / Robin Johnson.
Description: New York : Crabtree Publishing Company, 2019. |
  Series: Full steam ahead! | Includes index.
Identifiers: LCCN 2019023731 (print) | LCCN 2019023732 (ebook) |
  ISBN 9780778764090 (hardcover) |
  ISBN 9780778764595 (paperback) |
  ISBN 9781427123619 (ebook)
Subjects: LCSH: Mechanical engineering--Juvenile literature.
Classification: LCC TJ147 .J635 2019 (print) | LCC TJ147 (ebook) |
  DDC 621--dc23
LC record available at https://lccn.loc.gov/2019023731
LC ebook record available at https://lccn.loc.gov/2019023732

Printed in the U.S.A./102019/CG20190809

Table of Contents

Finding Solutions 4

On the Job 6

Meeting Needs 8

From All Sides 10

So Many Solutions! 12

Top Models 14

Pollution Problem 16

Different Energy 18

The Best Solution.... 20

Words to Know 22

Index and About the Author.... 23

Crabtree Plus Digital Code........... 23

STEAM Notes for Educators............... 24

Crabtree Publishing Company
www.crabtreebooks.com   1-800-387-7650
Copyright © **2020 CRABTREE PUBLISHING COMPANY**. All rights reserved. No part of this publication may be reproduced, stored in a retrieval system or be transmitted in any form or by any means, electronic, mechanical, photocopying, recording, or otherwise, without the prior written permission of Crabtree Publishing Company. In Canada: We acknowledge the financial support of the Government of Canada through the Book Publishing Industry Development Program (BPIDP) for our publishing activities.

Published in Canada
Crabtree Publishing
616 Welland Ave.
St. Catharines, Ontario
L2M 5V6

Published in the United States
Crabtree Publishing
PMB 59051
350 Fifth Avenue, 59th Floor
New York, New York 10118

Published in the United Kingdom
Crabtree Publishing
Maritime House
Basin Road North, Hove
BN41 1WR

Published in Australia
Crabtree Publishing
Unit 3 – 5 Currumbin Court
Capalaba
QLD 4157

Finding Solutions

What would you do if you needed to get across water? You could walk on a bridge. You could ride in a boat. Those are both solutions.

Bridges and boats are solutions for crossing over water. What is another solution?

A solution is an answer to a question or problem. Can you think of a time you found a solution?

This family's house was crowded with toys. Their solution is a toy basket. It helps keep the house clean!

On the Job

Some people have jobs finding solutions. They are called engineers. Engineers use math, science, and **creative thinking** to solve problems.

Engineers enjoy solving problems. They are always looking for new solutions. A new solution can solve a problem in a better or faster way.

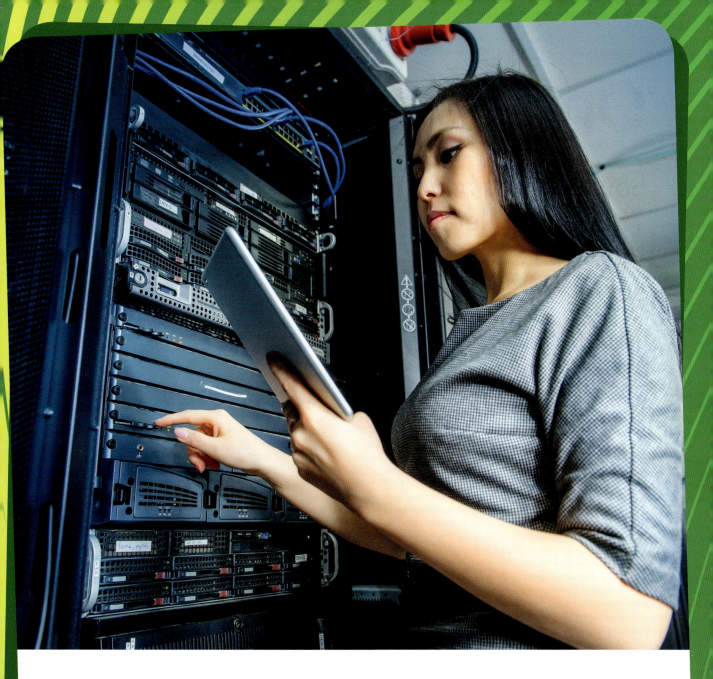

This engineer **designs** computers that make work easier. She makes sure they work as they should. She fixes any problems they have.

Meeting Needs

Engineers look for problems to solve. They find areas where **needs** are not being met. Engineers design things to meet those needs. They also design things that make life easier, safer, and more fun.

When there is not enough rain, plants cannot grow. This engineer solves the problem. She designs a way to bring water to plants.

Engineers designed all of these things! What problem does each item solve? How does it meet a need or make life easier, safer, or more fun?

From All Sides

Engineers find out as much as they can about a problem. They look at it from all sides. They study the problem up close. They find out how the problem **affects** people.

This engineer is climbing a ladder to study a problem up close.

This engineer found a problem with this road. It is damaged. He talked to people who use the road. He looks at the road up close.

So Many Solutions!

Engineers work together to solve problems. They **brainstorm** to think of as many solutions as they can. There are no wrong answers when you are brainstorming!

Working together helps engineers think of many different solutions.

This engineer wants to design shoes that will not slip on ice. He thinks of as many different solutions as he can.

These kids are brainstorming to design a way to reduce classroom waste.

Top Models

Engineers make **models** of their solutions. They test the models to see if they solve the problem. The tests show engineers how well their ideas will work. Then, engineers choose the best solution.

Tests help engineers find ways to improve their solutions. To improve is to make something better.

The best solution solves all parts of a problem or fully meets a need. Office workers had back pain after sitting all day. So engineers designed desks that would let them stand! The desks also move down to let them sit when they are tired.

Pollution Problem

Engineers look for ways to improve solutions. For example, engineers designed cars so we can travel quickly. But many cars use gas for **energy**. This **pollutes** the air. So engineers look for ways to solve the problem.

Engineers designed cars to solve the problem of slow travel. They have improved the first designs over time.

Engineers work together to design cars that do not use gas.

Engineers use models to make and test new car designs.

Different Energy

Engineers have many ideas for cars that do not use gas. They design cars that get energy from the Sun. They design cars that run on wind power. They make and test models to find the best solution.

These models are powered by the Sun. Large panels collect the Sun's energy.

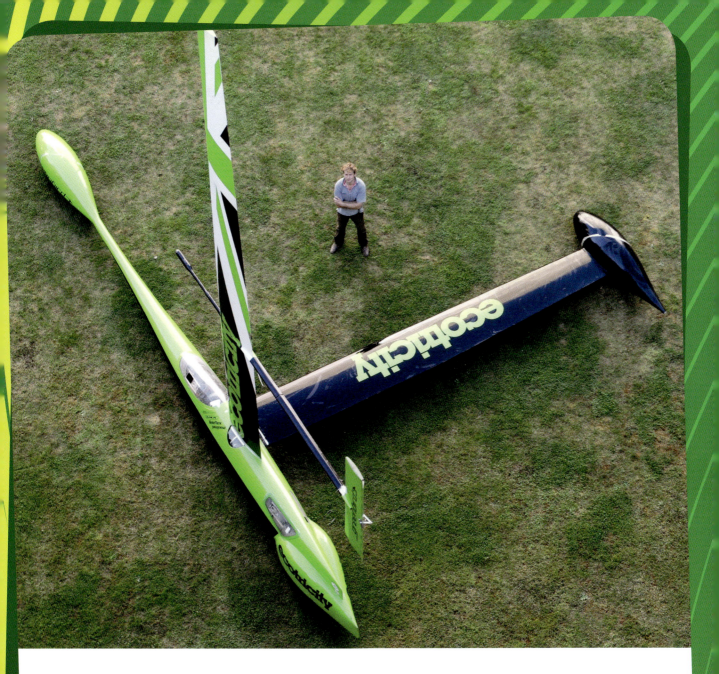

This model runs on wind energy. Air flows over sails on the car and pushes it forward.

The Best Solution

After testing many models, engineers found the best solution. They design cars that run on **electricity**. Drivers plug these cars in to give them power.

These engineers are testing an electric car to make sure it works well.

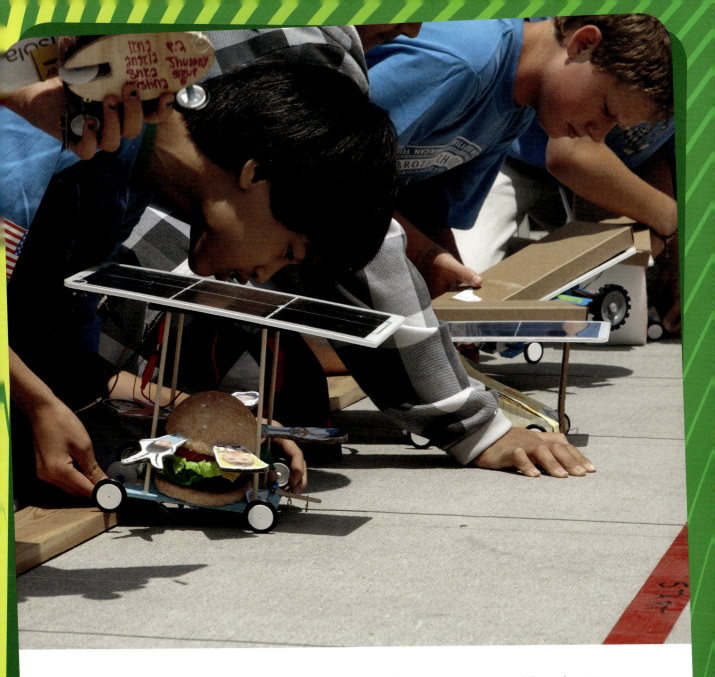

You can find solutions too! These kids made cars powered by the Sun. They are racing their models to test them.

Words to Know

affects [*uh*-FEKTS] verb Makes an impact on

brainstorm [BREYN-stawrm] verb To work together to share many ideas on a subject

creative thinking [kree-EY-tiv THING-king] noun Using your mind to make up new and original ideas

designs [dih-ZAHYNS] verb Makes a plan to create something

electricity [ih-lek-TRIS-i-tee] noun A type of energy that provides power, such as light

energy [EN-er-jee] noun The power to do work

models [MOD-ls] noun Representations of real objects

needs [needs] noun Things we need to survive

pollutes [*puh*-LOOTS] verb Makes dirty

A noun is a person, place, or thing.

A verb is an action word that tells you what someone or something does.

An adjective is a word that tells you what something is like.

Index

brainstorm 12–13
cars 16–21
electricity 20
engineers 6–18, 20
improve 14, 16
models 14, 17–21

needs 8–9
problems 5–17
Sun energy 18, 21
testing 14–15, 17–21
wind energy 19

About the Author

Robin Johnson is a freelance author and editor who has written more than 80 children's books. When she isn't working, Robin builds castles in the sky with her engineer husband and their two best creations—sons Jeremy and Drew.

To explore and learn more, enter the code at the Crabtree Plus website below.

www.crabtreeplus.com/fullsteamahead

Your code is:
fsa20

STEAM Notes for Educators

Full STEAM Ahead is a literacy series that helps readers build vocabulary, fluency, and comprehension while learning about big ideas in STEAM subjects. *What is the Best Solution?* allows readers to use evidence from the text to find answers to questions about how engineers find the best solutions. The STEAM activity below helps readers extend the ideas in the book to build their skills in engineering and language arts.

My Solution Story

Children will be able to:
- Understand that there are many solutions to one problem, and that engineers find the best solution through brainstorming and testing.
- Create a story with pictures and captions that shows how engineers found the best solution.

Materials
- My Solution Story Worksheet
- My Solution Story Completed Example
- Technology to use as story prompt, such as a helmet, a refrigerator, or an alarm clock (Use a picture or a physical object.)

Guiding Prompts
After reading *What is the Best Solution?*, ask children:
- What do engineers do?
- How do engineers find solutions?

Activity Prompts
Explain to children they will help tell the story of how engineers found a solution we use every day. Show children the technology that will be used as a story prompt. Explain that engineers designed it to solve a problem or meet a need. Ask them:
- What problem does this solve?/What need does this meet?

Go through completed example with children based on the technology chosen.

Then, show them a new technology and hand each child the My Solution Story Worksheet. They will fill in the worksheet, completing the story of how the pair of engineers came up with a solution. They will illustrate pictures and write short sentences or words to fill in blanks. Children can get creative with their solutions!

Have children present their stories to their peers. Create a large, class list of the many different solutions that children came up with in their stories. Discuss how there are many solutions to the same problem. Ask children how they decided on the best solution in their story. Share the strategies they used to narrow down the best idea, and discuss how engineers in the real world would then test and improve this idea.

Extensions
- Use the engineering design process to find the best solution to a classroom problem.

To view and download the worksheet, visit **www.crabtreebooks.com/resources/ printables** or **www.crabtreeplus.com/ fullsteamahead** and enter the code **fsa20**.